Art Against Forgetting

PAINTINGS BY LEONARD MEISELMAN

Essays by Donald Kuspit and Susan Chevlowe

Exhibition Curated by Reba Wulkan

YESHIVA UNIVERSITY MUSEUM

Center for Jewish History

15 West 16th Street New York, NY 10011

JUNE 13–OCTOBER 13, 2002

"...Art is in order not to die of the truth..."

—NIETZSCHE

For Survivors Everywhere

The Yeshiva University Museum takes pride in exhibiting "Art Against Forgetting." Leonard Meiselman deals with two motifs that are especially meaningful to American Jews: prayer shawls and American flags, both filled with ritual and ceremony.

The artist portrays the fragmented portions of prayer shawls, weathered, beaten, but never completely destroyed. Prayer shawls represent man's attempt to control his destiny; indeed, they follow man to his grave. As in the refrain of the Yiddish song my mother sang to me: "*Ales, ales, nor dem Tales....*" At death, everything is taken away from an individual but his Tallit. Meiselman's American flags are equally scarred but remain symbols of pride, nationalism, and triumph. These artworks are veils that, in their verticality, hide reality and protect the sacred within.

It is particularly appropriate to exhibit this body of work at the Yeshiva University Museum which is dedicated to enriching and interpreting Jewish life. The Museum would like to acknowledge the support of the New York City Department of Cultural Affairs, the New York State Council on the Arts, and the Smart Family Foundation.

—REBA WULKAN, Contemporary Exhibitions Curator, 2002

I wish to express my gratitude to Sylvia A. Herskowitz, Museum Director, Reba Wulkan, Contemporary Exhibitions Curator, and the Yeshiva University Museum for making this exhibition possible. We need to express ourselves in order to be individuals. We need to share ideas and communicate in order to be a community. The Yeshiva University Museum, in providing a forum for contemporary issues, serves the community in the way we always hoped and believed museums would.

—LEONARD MEISELMAN

Prayer Shawl From Auschwitz, 2000.
Oil on canvas, 40x60 in.

Against Forgetting, 2000. Oil on canvas, 40x60 in.

Kaddish, 2000.
Oil on canvas, 40x60 in.

Self, 2000.
Oil on canvas, 40x60 in.

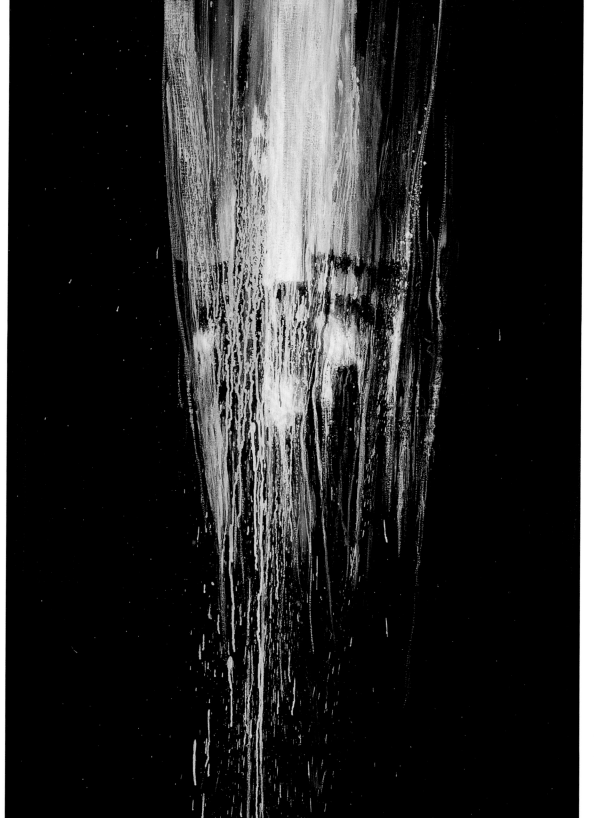

Weeping May Endure, 2001.
Oil on canvas, 40x60 in.

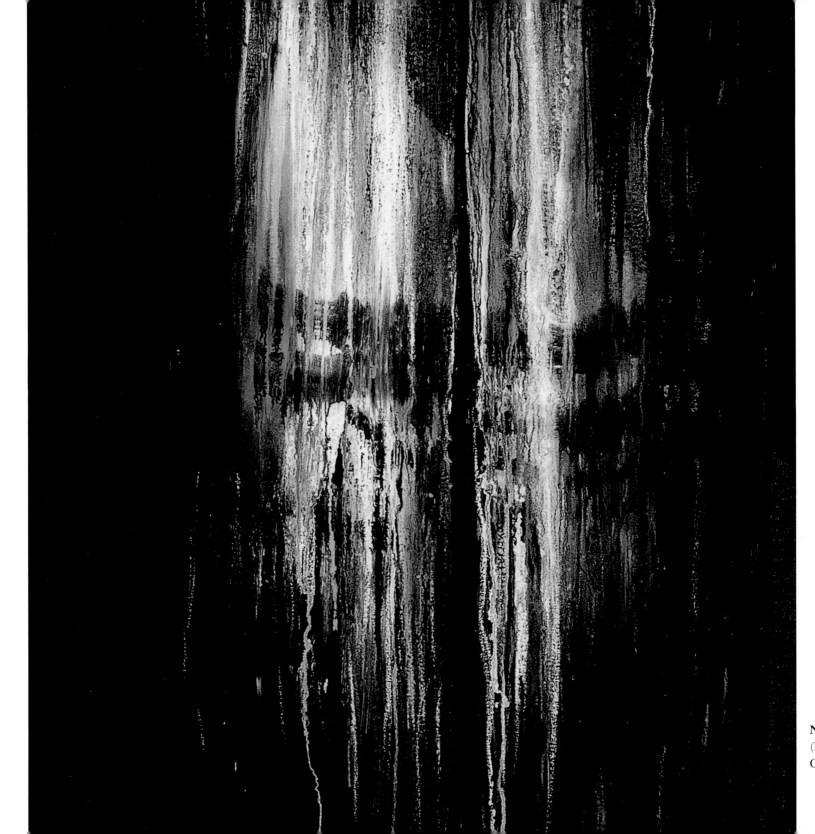

"Then a spirit passed before my face…" Job 4:15

No One Should Speak
(Detail), 2001.
Oil on canvas, 40x60 in.

Death Excitement: Leonard Meiselman's Paintings

BY DONALD KUSPIT

Restated in terms of instincts, ugliness—destruction—
is the expression of the death instinct;
beauty—the desire to unite into rhythms and wholes—
is that of the life instinct.

The achievement of the artist is in giving the fullest
expression to the conflict and the union between these two.

Hanna Segal,
A Psychoanalytic Approach to Aesthetics

Leonard Meiselman is an expressionist painter, and what he expresses, in the very surface of his paintings, is death, more particularly the all but overwhelming anxiety—the terrifying excitement—it arouses in us. Meiselman is obsessed with death, not just the everyday death of people who have lived their God-given three score and ten years, if not longer, but man-made death, the inhumanity that leads to premature death, that cuts people off in the prime of their life, and even murders innocent children. Why shouldn't he be, for in the last century there was more mass murder than ever before, greater indifference to life on a greater scale than the world has ever known before? It began with the stalemate of trench warfare, in which opposing armies fought each other to a meaningless death, climaxed with the destruction of the Jews in the Holocaust—a vicious event that became symbolic of the suffering that has left its stain on every century—and gathered fresh momentum with the destruction of the World Trade Center at the beginning of this century. Meiselman's paintings of Jewish prayer shawls and the tattered American flag are poignant reminders of these last events.

The paintings are as disturbing as the events themselves. They are existential memento mori that concentrate, in a single image, indeed, a single object, painted with agonizing emotional realism—a brilliant mix of gesturalism and realism, in which painterly gestures seem to dissolve the real object, which nonetheless survives in ghostly form— their destructiveness. Meiselman's paint becomes the acid of death eating through life, leaving behind a mournful, horrific reminder of tragedy and loss. We usually repress our anxiety about death—annihilative anxiety, expressive of our own destructiveness as well as our fear of destruction—but Meiselman takes it out of its hiding place in the unconscious, exposing it through his forceful, and fearless, painterliness. It preserves what is left of life even as it announces its death. He looks death in the eye, and his eye never blinks, because it is full of instinctive life, ironically evident in the fatal gestures.

Against Forgetting and *Kaddish*, along with other prayer shawl paintings, and the two versions of *Flag from Ground Zero*, are not only powerfully painted, as their gestural turbulence indicates—it tersely conveys the emotional as well as physical disintegration the victims suffered—but iconographically original. Meiselman paints the Triumph of Death, but where Death is traditionally conceived as the anonymous remains of a human figure, Meiselman's prayer shawl and American flag symbolize Death, becoming in effect figures—symbols that convey all too human emotion, indeed, that seem more poignantly human and expressive than any human being. Meiselman's prayer shawls and flags thus become uncannily intimate and personal. His signature painting certainly personalizes them, but so does the fact that they are culturally specific, each evoking a particular people and their ideals. The Jewish prayer shawl and the American flag are sacred emblems— God has blessed America as well as the Jews, which is why both represent a higher truth and the possibility of a better life than are ordinarily available on earth—and continue to be so in Meiselman's paintings, however profaned by death. Meiselman's Triumphs of Death take us a step beyond those of Hans Baldung-Grien and Hans Holbein. In Meiselman, Death—morbid decay, conveying inevitable misery—is not only pictured but ingrained in the image's texture, which gets under one's skin—one is infected by it, as it were—while retaining its collective significance. Meiselman's irksome gesturalism—the tortured painterly skin of his images—gives his paintings an air of explosive panic beyond anything imagined by the German masters.

In fact, Meiselman's prayer shawls and flags are spiritual skins that have been stripped from living bodies. They are frayed but still intact—recognizable if ruined.

Meiselman's handling seems to shred them in rage—they in fact look like they have been through a shredder, as their striated appearance suggests—even as it conveys their abandoned condition. They are like the imprints of Christ on the Turin shroud and Veronica's napkin—mysterious stains marking the surface of the canvas with the victim's appearance, as barely decipherable as the mystery of his sacred being and painful death, of which they are the aborted memories. Indeed, Meiselman's paintings are about being and nothingness—how nothingness dwells within being, and is released by suffering, but also how nothingness gives being more presence. Meiselman's prayer shawls and flags have a startling presence, by reason of the insistence and intensity with which Meiselman paints them, and because of their isolation in the darkness, which puts them beyond consolation. Meiselman is painting the two sides of his identity: he is Jewish and American. They converge in his self-portraits, which show the same acute consciousness of suffering and death—the same agony—as his symbolic portraits of the Holocaust and America. (Both his prayer shawls and American flags are survivors, or rather artifacts that symbolize the victims, more particularly, the cremation by fire that links them. The former are based on a photograph of a pile of prayer shawls confiscated by the Nazis at Auschwitz and the latter on a photograph of an American flag found at Ground Zero.) In the *September 11, 2001* collage he screams—in a self-portrait *(Myself)*, repeated as though amplifying the scream and destroyed, as though Meiselman was a victim of the event—with even greater agony than the figure in Munch's *The Scream*. For Meiselman has witnessed two Holocausts, and his scream is their witness, while Munch has only witnessed his own mental derangement, that is, testifies to his own insanity, rather than the insanity of the world. In another self-portrait he stares out at us from behind a painterly veil or shroud, haunting us like the ghost of one of the victims. He clearly identifies with them, which is why he is no silent witness—he must scream as they could not , scream for them, express their suffering in public as they could not, express the agony of their death throes stifled by the indifference and contempt of the Nazis.

Ironically, the unrelenting black and blood red that Meiselman uses in many of his portraits—perhaps most noteworthily in *Self-Portrait with Father*—and in several of the prayer shawl pictures are the colors of the Nazi flag, where they symbolize power rather than pain. This suggests that Meiselman, while identifying with the dead victims of the September 11th and Jewish Holocausts, also suffers from survivor's guilt. Meiselman has studied many faces, and he always finds the "inner face" behind them, to use the psychoanalyst Michael's Eigen's phrase. It is invariably melancholy, as his portraits of Martin Buber—his humanistic father figure—but also grim, as his abstract portraits—marvellous studies in psychological realism, for all their abstractness—indicate. All of Meiselman's portraits are introspective—acutely aware of inner life, psychodynamic as well as sociodynamic, like the best expressionism—but none more deeply than the abstract portraits.

They dramatize the psyche, conveying the dialectic of annihilative anxiety and cosmic ecstasy at its core, indicating that Meiselman, however engrossed in death and destruction, also yearns for integration, for the heads are self-contained wholes however grotesquely distorted. Split, even fragmented—all but shattered—they nonetheless hold together (as the frame around the head in *Witness* emphasizes). They are portraits of a troubled, tortured integrity, but integrity it is nonetheless. If, as Hanna Segal writes, beauty involves "the desire to unite into rhythms and wholes," then Meiselman's abstract portraits— lined up in a row, they seem to trace the stages of the self's disintegration, what looks like a passionate whirlpool slowly but surely becoming a desperate abyss—are oddly beautiful rhythmic wholes. The philosopher Francis Bacon said that all beauty has something strange in it—something ugly and destructive, referring again to the Segal epigraph—and Meiselman has brought out the destructive ugliness in beauty (and the self) with no loss of wholeness, however shaken it may be. The abstract heads show the conflict be between the death and life instincts that rages within Meiselman. (His art is clearly a projection of his inner life.) They seamlessly unite, indeed, seem, paradoxically, one and the same, in his marvelous drawings, where each rhythmic line is full of instinctive life, and as such death-defying and whole in itself, while at the same readable as a cutting edge—

a fatal incision in organic form that at the same time defines it. The same perplexing union of death and life instincts—of painful anguish and ecstatic exuberance (antithetical emotions seem the same at their most intense)—is evident in Meiselman's paintings of whales and trees, although in them the balance is tilted to life rather than death.

Theodor Adorno has famously argued that it is barbaric to make art after Auschwitz, which is pure negativity become socially actual. But Meiselman shows that it is still necessary, however barbaric the intense expressivity of the art that results may look, that is, however much it reflects, and thus seems to temper, the barbarism of the events it acknowledges. Especially when it acknowledges the disaster of Auschwitz—brings to artistic life the death that it is—and similar Holocausts. Adorno's idea is intellectually interesting, but beside the human point, as Meiselman indicates. He shows that one must try to paint—articulate, art, at the least, being a mode of intense, commemorative articulation—the impossible but real, especially because its impossibility makes it real, and the most interesting and engaging art is ultimately about the mystery of the impossible become real, the strangeness of the incomprehensible actually occurring, that is, "realized" in both the inner and outer worlds. As Meiselman's scream suggests the time for silent, passive witnessing of man's inhumanity to man is over. Anti-Semitism and anti-Americanism are on the rise yet again—they will probably always be with us—and it is high time to give voice to our horror and anger at them, which is what Meiselman's profound paintings do. It is a sign of life to do so. The death instinct may be alive and well in Leonard Meiselman's paintings, but so, with an aggressive power more than equal to it, is the life instinct. All his works are an effort to find meaning in death—especially in mass death, which makes it seem all the more meaningless—and the meaning he has found is that it contains life, unexpectedly.

DONALD KUSPIT is an art critic and professor of art history and philosophy at the State University of New York at Stony Brook. He is the editor of *Art Criticism* and contributing editor at *Art Forum*, *Sculpture* and *New Art Examiner* magazines. Kuspit's books include *Psychostrategies of Avant-Garde Art* (Cambridge University Press, 2002).

Sept. 11, 2001, 2001.
Collage, 9x24 in.

Flag from Ground Zero, I,
2001. Oil on canvas, 31x47 in.

Flag from Ground Zero, II, 2001.
Oil on canvas, 40x60 in.

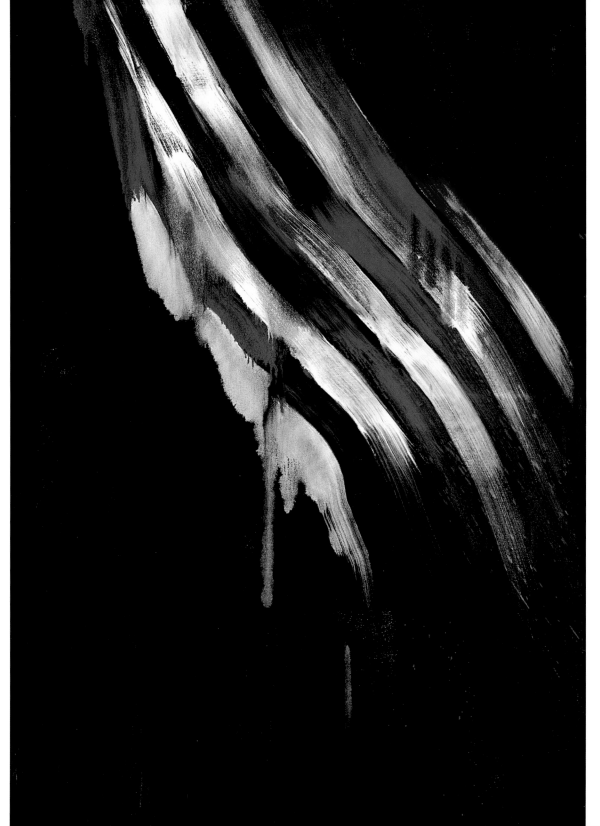

Flag from Ground Zero, III, 2002.
Oil on canvas, 40x60 in.

Flag from Ground Zero, IV, 2002.
Oil on canvas, 40x60 in.

PAINTING, LEARNING & SURVIVING

by Leonard Meiselman

Whenever I feel confused and hurt, I try to get into my studio. If I can make some marks with paint or pencil I can get closer to my feelings and I seem to understand things better. The process of painting reveals me to myself.

I PAINT IN ORDER TO LEARN.

My mother died in 1987 and my mother's death pains me still. I have been painting canvases called *Goodbye Mother* for fourteen years now, trying to get closer to understanding the reality of her life and death.

LEARNING HOW TO LIVE WITH HOW LITTLE I KNOW.

I have never understood the enormity of the Holocaust.

In 1999 an "abstract" form on a canvas seemed to resemble a prayer shawl.

It appeared at first pale and tentative. It appeared like a vision or an opportunity for dialogue. It asked to be realized. It required to be painted. A souvenir from my darkest imaginings. I began at once impulsively trying to conjure it up—in dabs and drippings of paint—it seemed to be painting itself.

It seemed familiar and inevitable.

Demanding and necessary. Appropriate and essential. A deja vu. Painting followed painting for three years with more and more complex histories and emotions about the Holocaust becoming real to me.

I APPROACH EACH NEW PAINTING WITH AWE—TERROR—AND REVERENCE.

I seem to need to paint these paintings. They are elegies for the past.

I feel like I am saying prayers with paint brushes.

Terribly alone and not alone. The paint raining down like tears from my brush.

September 11th happened and seems to go on happening in my mind like the Holocaust does.

A FLAG WAS FOUND AT GROUND ZERO. I saw it on TV It was torn and burned. It seemed like another kind of prayer shawl. Intuitively I thought I could paint it. It's possible that it wasn't torn or burned and I imagined it that way or felt it to be that way—hurt—and violated. I started painting red, white and blue for the first time ever and I realized how my response to the flag had changed after Sept. 11th.

Flag and prayer shawl. Symbols that marked many for death—symbols of faith that survives. Symbols I inherit and that mark me.

PRAYER SHAWL BECAME A FLAG, FLAG BECAME A PRAYER SHAWL.

Impossible to make art out of such tragedy. It is impossible not to.

I don't know how I could go on living without placing the colors and the brush strokes in my own path so that I can stumble over them and weep—finally—and pick myself up.

THE PRAYER IN MY PAINTINGS—THE RAGE AND THE TEARS—ARE INSIDE ME.

When I am painting is when I am most alive.

These paintings have taught me how connected we are to each other and to echoes and vibrations that call out to us from injustice from events that impinge upon the definition of our lives and identities. These paintings have taught me, as an artist, how we all require symbols and forms to express our destiny, our needs, and our mutual despair. We need paintings and poems to help us survive in the world and to become who we are.

Asked why I do these paintings I respond "I do not know".
I realize that I don't understand why. These paintings are a work-in-progress. Awkward notes or sketches for a work ahead.

My art is about life and death and learning.   HOW I RESPOND TELLS ME ABOUT WHO I AM.
I CONTINUE TO LEARN WHAT'S INSIDE ME.

These paintings are a diary of learning moments. A journal of reaching in and reaching out. Learning how to respond—how to survive—how to care for and express that glowing inner truth of ourselves—as we seek for meaning, purpose and the courage to continue.

L.M. Feb 2002

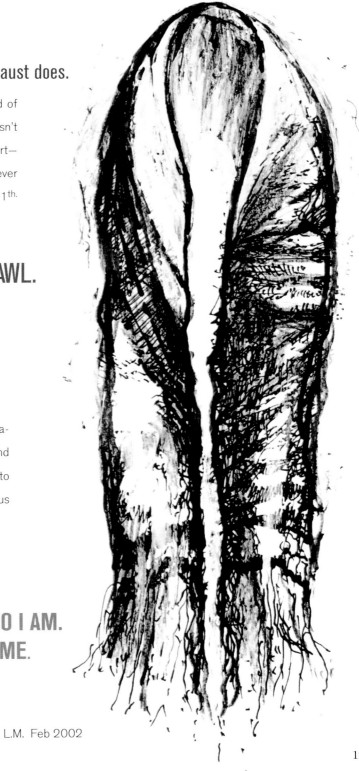

In Search Of Martin Buber, 1992.
Pencil, 39x42 in.

A Declaration of Faith

BY SUSAN CHEVLOWE

Life and death. Presence and absence. We live our lives negotiating the awesome pathways defined by these inexorable contradictions. Leonard Meiselman's paintings of traditional shawls (*tallit*) worn by observant Jews during prayer are palpable researches into these mysteries. Each canvas depicts a single *tallit*, suggesting both the enigma of God's Oneness and the loneliness of the individual.

In the late 1990s, while painting abstractly, an image emerged on Meiselman's canvas that would become a dominant preoccupation for the next several years: the *tallit*. "It was hanging; it was torn," Meiselman recalls thinking. "I thought it could be a prayer shawl from Auschwitz—the last things the victims had that were part of their lives; their last contact with their culture." Dealing with the subject of the Holocaust was not unfamiliar to him. "I had been working on Holocaust themes for forty years," Meiselman said.[1]

In Meiselman's paintings, the *tallit* blanches white against a dark background whose depth is unknowable. On some canvases, the paint drips, like flowing milk or thickened tears. The prayer shawl represents an index of what is absent—the living human being to whom it once belonged. At the same time, its emptiness raises the question of the absence of God himself, a problem that has dogged both Jewish and Christian theologians since the Holocaust. Where was God at Auschwitz? Since the mid-1960s, this challenge, and its place within the larger inquiry into the nature of God and his relationship to human beings, continue to be at the core of Holocaust theology. The question was also raised anew in the context of the terrorist attacks at the World Trade Center and the Pentagon: Where was God on September 11? Meiselman explores these consequences in the series "Flag from Ground Zero" and in other recent canvases, where the *tallit* and flag dissolve into one another.

Artists who wrestle with the depiction of mass death often focus on the suffering of one individual. Such an approach resonates in both Christian and Jewish theology. In the Christian view, this is most obvious in the suffering of Jesus. Such artists as Rico Lebrun (1900-1964) and Zoran Music (1909-), working in the 1950s and in the 1970s, respectively, sought, it could be said, to recover meaning from the brutalized and violated human form, in Lebrun's words, "by changing what is disfigured into what is transfigured."

Such depictions commonly demonstrate the tension between graphic representations of human suffering and the propensity toward abstraction. For Meiselman, who was painting abstractly at the time the image of the *tallit* emerged, that tension is evident as well. The *tallit* manifested almost unconsciously, as if derived from his own studies of the Jewish theologian and philosopher Martin Buber (1878-1965), who had been a powerful influence on Meiselman's thinking. Buber's concept of "I /Thou," what he calls the primary word, posits being as relationship—between human beings themselves, between the individual and God, and between everything in nature, animate or not. "I was trying to paint what Buber was trying to say," Meiselman has said. In several drawings and in a painting of Buber entitled "Ecstasy," 1985, the head is a swirling vortex, not unlike the whirlwind of destruction in the Book of Job.[2]

The magnetism of Buber's thinking, which itself was influenced by research into eastern European Hasidic culture, resonates in Meiselman's use of the *tallit* as both a symbol of Oneness and of the struggle inherent in the I/Thou relationship.[3] "We are divine, we are alive because of a miracle. In one vein of my work that is what I am approaching. If you can't prove it then it's mystical and you can only believe in it," the artist says.

The *tallit* acquires its significance as a holy object by virtue of the fringes (*tzitzit*) attached to its four corners. During prayer, the wearer often touches the fringes as a specific reminder of God and the commandments. Observant Jews learn, "When you put on a *tallit* you should think that the Light of the Infinite One is hidden within this *tallit* that you wrap yourself in…and that when the wings of the *tallit* cover you, you are covered in the wings of the Light of the Infinite One."[4] The intensity of the *tallit's* symbolism is related in this Hasidic tale about Rabbi Nachman of Bratzlav:

> The *rebbe* once gave his old *tallit* to one of his close followers, someone on a high level, and told him, "Be careful to treat this *tallit* with respect and honor. You should know that as many threads as there are in this *tallit*, that is how many tears I shed before God until I understood what a *tallit* is."[5]

The prayer shawl was an authentic part of Meiselman's synagogue experience growing up in the Bronx, New York, in the aftermath of the destruction of European Jewry. Yet, the artist belongs to a generation that recited the Hebrew liturgy by rote with little comprehension of the depth of its meaning. Even so, the tactile sensation of the *tallit* transmitted that mystical connection to the Infinite that more observant Jews, and, indeed, the Hasidim, traditionally may know.

During the artist's childhood, the unworn *tallit* may have symbolized the unspoken pang of absence marking a silence about the Holocaust. In the late 1980s, the subject of the *tallit* resurfaced, in a series of paintings called *Goodbye Mother*—meditations on the illness and death of the artist's mother. Later, as Meiselman was working on a series he calls *Self-Portrait with Father*, September 11 happened. The World Trade Center site in effect became a mass grave for the nearly three thousand victims who lost their lives when two hijacked planes were intentionally crashed into the Twin Towers. Soon after the rescue efforts began, an American flag was found at Ground Zero. The process of memorializing these deaths continues to involve an entire nation that has frequently taken comfort in the stars and stripes. Sentiments vacillate between shared feelings of countrywide mourning and unity and the intense isolation of personal grief and disruption. For Meiselman, this progression has become bound up with the unfathomability of the Holocaust and the reality of his father's closeness to death. His father has insisted that his son say Kaddish when he dies but Meiselman admits he does not know how. Out of this anxiety, he addressed the subject in a painting imagining himself saying Kaddish.

Rabbi Hayim Halevy Donin writes of the significance of the Kaddish—the word itself means Holy—as "an act of reverence for a deceased parent." He describes how the "Kaddish is not technically a prayer for the dead….It makes no reference to the dead or to mourning. It is a prayer in praise of God. It is a declaration of deep faith in the exalted greatness of the Almighty and a petition for ultimate redemption and salvation." An ancient prayer, it was during the early Middle Ages that the Kaddish became identified with mourners. Rabbi Donin explains, "If, in the midst of grief and personal loss, when the tendency to blame and reject God might arise, a person nevertheless rises publicly to express these words of faith and trust in God—this is an act of great merit to the soul of the deceased, for the deceased is credited with having raised a child capable of such an act of faith. In this sense only can the Kaddish be regarded as an indirect 'prayer for the dead.'"[6]

Meiselman's painting *Kaddish*, 2000, brings to mind the great British modernist painter David Bomberg's *Hear O Israel*, 1955. Both highly expressionistic self-portraits are powerful affirmations of faith and intimate the presence of the divine even in the face of death. *Hear O Israel* takes its title from the biblical passage known as the Shema (in English, "Hear") that observant Jews recite twice a day.[7] Like the Kaddish the Shema also is not a prayer. According to Rabbi Donin, "*It is a declaration of faith*. It is an affirmation of the unity of God…."[8]

Life and death. Presence and absence. These dilemmas are at the core of Holocaust theology. Where is God? While, according to Meiselman, after September 11 "American Jews are survivors twice," the scholar of Holocaust memoir David Patterson asserts that the survivor's "desire for God is without end even when God reveals himself as absence rather than presence." And the theologian Eliezer Schweid states, "Jews must take responsibility for the enigma of the Jewish believer's loneliness before a hiding God."[9]

Meiselman's paintings have an important message, too. He tells us: "Despite the fact that we are survivors, there is an inner light, an ecstasy, a euphoria, a passionate thrill to be alive."

SUSAN CHEVLOWE is an art historian and former Associate Curator of Fine Arts at The Jewish Museum, New York. She is the author of *Common Man, Mythic Vision: The Paintings of Ben Shahn* (Princeton University Press, 1998) and co-edited *Painting A Place in America: Jewish Artists in New York, 1900-1945* (Indiana Press, 1991).

"9/11", 2002.
Oil on canvas, 40x60 in.

[1] The artist in conversation with the author, January 23, 2002, Port Washington, New York. All quotations from the artist were taken from this conversation. Meiselman refers specifically to having worked on the acclaimed architect Louis Kahn's project for a memorial to the six million Jewish victims of the Holocaust. Comprised of six glass towers, the monument was originally planned for a site in lower Manhattan but never built.

[2] See Dan Cohn-Sherbok, *Holocaust Theology: A Reader* (Exeter, United Kingdom: Exeter University Press, 2002). <www.ex.ac.uk/uep/HolocaustIntro.htm>. The eminent scholar of Holocaust theology Dan Cohn-Sherbok notes the importance of the Book of Job as a continuing precedent for understanding God and the Holocaust. In his Introduction to *Holocaust Theology*, Cohn-Sherbok points to Rabbi Irving Greenberg, who "stresses that the image of Job is of central importance in attempting to make sense of this tragedy. Modern Jews, he argues, should attempt to model themselves on Job's example. Like Job, they should recognize that there are no easy pieties which explain away the perplexities posed by the Holocaust. What is important about the biblical account is that Job demonstrates that God's presence is manifest in the whirlwind and that contact with God can be restored despite suffering and death."

[3] In the essay "Hasidism and Modern Man" (1958), Buber wrote: "Hasidic teaching says that the worlds could fulfill their destiny of becoming one by virtue of the life of man becoming one. But how is that to be understood? Is not a complete unity of living being inconceivable except in God himself?…Man cannot approach the divine by going beyond the human. But he can approach it by becoming the man that he, this individual man, was created to become. This seems to me the eternal essence of Hasidic Life and Hasidic teaching." Martin Buber, "Hasidism and Modern Man," originally published in A. Altmann, ed. *Between East and West*, (London, 1958). Excerpt reprinted in Nathan N. Glatzer, ed., *The Way of Response: Martin Buber*. (New York: Schocken Books, 1966), 195.

[4] *Or ha-Ganuz l'Tzaddikim* (Jerusalem, 1966), 36. Quoted in Yitzhak Buxbaum, *Jewish Spiritual Practices* (Northvale, New Jersey, and London: Jason Aronson Inc., 1994), 105-6.

[5] *Sichot ha-Ran*, in *Hishtapchut ha-Nefesh* (Jerusalem, 1976), 19. Quoted in Buxbaum, *Jewish Spiritual Practices*, 105.

[6] Rabbi Hayim Halevy Donin, *To be a Jew* (New York: Basic Books, 1991), 304-7.

[7] Recited in Hebrew, the Shema is translated as follows: "Hear O Israel, the Lord is God, the Lord is One. Blessed be the name of his glorious Majesty forever and ever. Love the Lord your God with all your heart, with all your soul, with all your means. And these words which I command you today shall be upon your heart. Teach them diligently to your children, and talk of them when you sit in your house, when you walk on the road, when you lie down and when you rise up. Bind them for a sign upon your hand and for frontlets between your eyes. Write them upon the doorposts of your house and upon your gates." Quoted in Donin, *To be a Jew*, 164.

[8] Ibid.

[9] Dan Cohn-Sherbok, *Holocaust Theology: A Reader* (Exeter, United Kingdom: Exeter University Press, 2002). <www.ex.ac.uk/uep/HolocaustIntro.htm>. See also David Patterson, *Sun Turned to Darkness* (Syracuse, New York: Syracuse University Press, 1998) and Eliezer Schweid, *Wrestling Until Day-Break* (Lanham, Maryland: University Press of America, 1994).

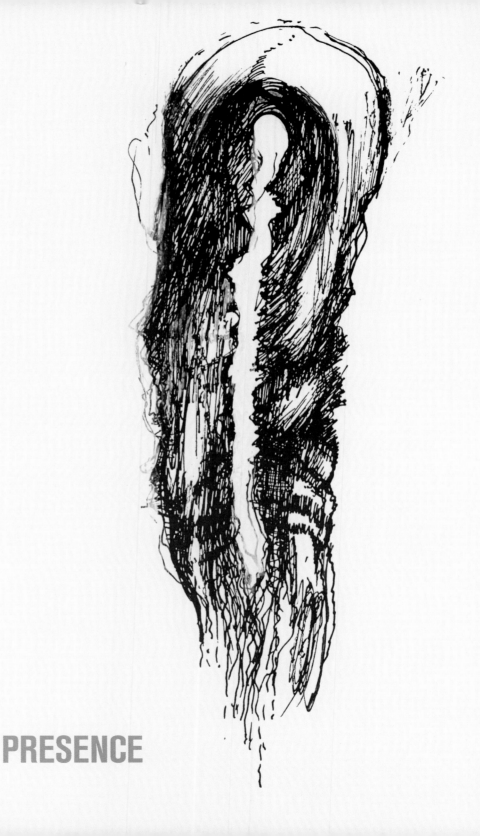

PRESENCE

PRAYER

Self Portrait Saying Kaddish, 2000.
Oil on canvas, 28x36 in.

"This is the Eternal Source of Art: a man is faced by a form which desires to be made through him into a work. This form is no offspring of his soul, but is an appearance which steps up to it and demands of it the effective power. The man is concerned with an act of his being. If he carries it through, if he speaks the primary word out of his being to the form which appears, then the effective powers streams out, and the work arises."

—MARTIN BUBER, *I and Thou*

Myself, 2001.
Oil on canvas, 40x60 in.

Self Portrait with Father, 2001.
Oil on canvas, 40x60 in.

Ecstasy. 1985.
Oil on canvas, 40x60 in.

"It lies with yourself how much of the immeasurable becomes reality for you."

—MARTIN BUBER.

The Miracle, 2001.
Pencil, 30x50 in.

No One Should Speak, 2001.
Oil on canvas, 40x60 in.

1997-1999

I lived on a hilltop near Florence, Italy from 1969 to 1987.

I began a series of whale paintings during that time.

I also had a compelling visual experience of trees

in Tuscany. I moved back to New York in 1989 and

continued with the whale series. I began painting *Whale,*

1999 in 1997 and completed it in 1999. In 1998

I began my first attempt to revisit my Tree experience

in a series of large pencil and pastel drawings.

—LM

Tree Vision I, 1998.
Pencil and pastel, 38 x 50 in.

Whale, 1999.
Oil on canvas, 53x80 in.

Above, **Tree-Vision, II**, 1998.
Pencil & pastel, 44x59 in.

Right, **Tree-Vision, II** (Detail).

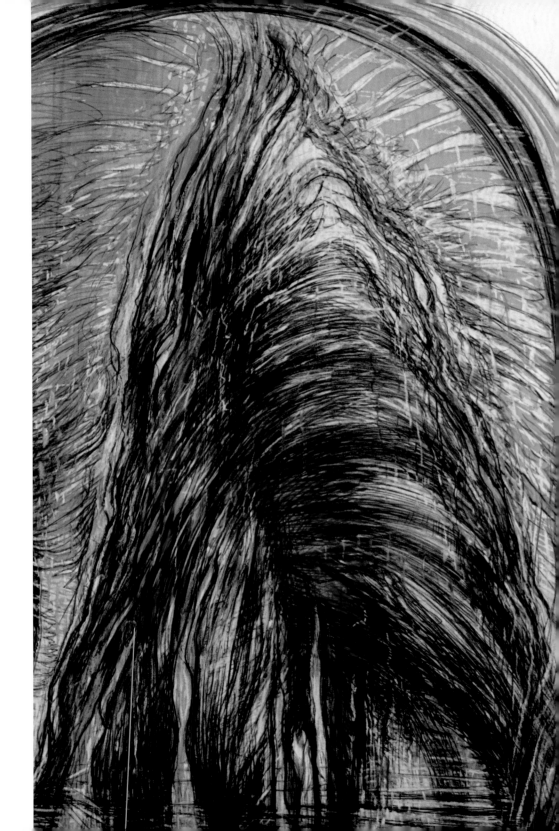

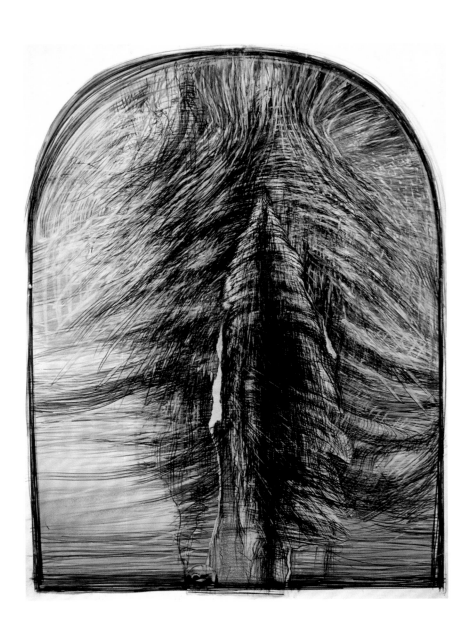

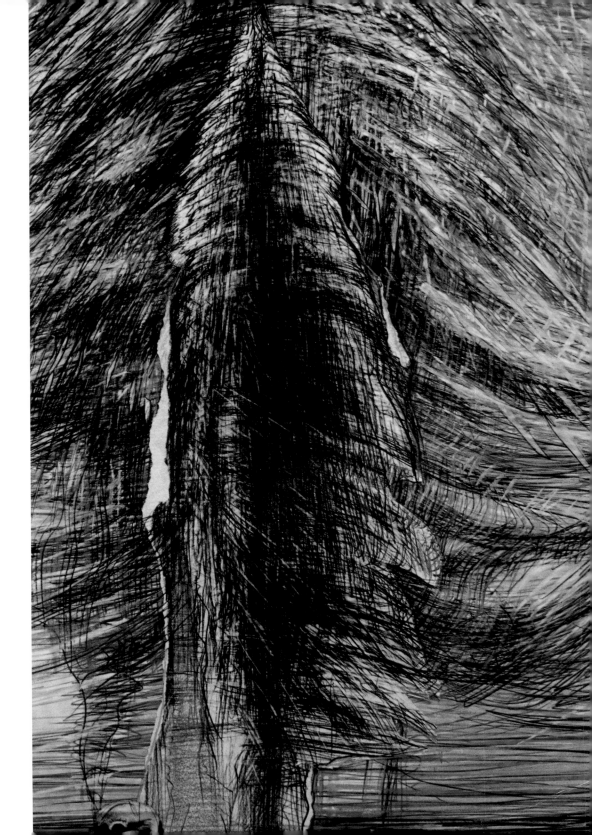

Above, **Tree-Vision, III**, 1998.
Pencil & pastel, 44x59 in.

Right, **Tree-Vision, III** (Detail).

Left, **Creature**, 1997. Oil, 53x80 in.

Opposite, clockwise from top left,
Tzaddik, 1986. Oil, 28x35 in.,
The World, 1989. Oil, 40x60 in.,
Survivor, 1985. Oil, 32x48 in.,
S.H., 1998. Pencil, 38x50 in.,
Witness, 2001. Pencil, 28x39 in.,
Creature, 1999. Pencil, 18x24 in.

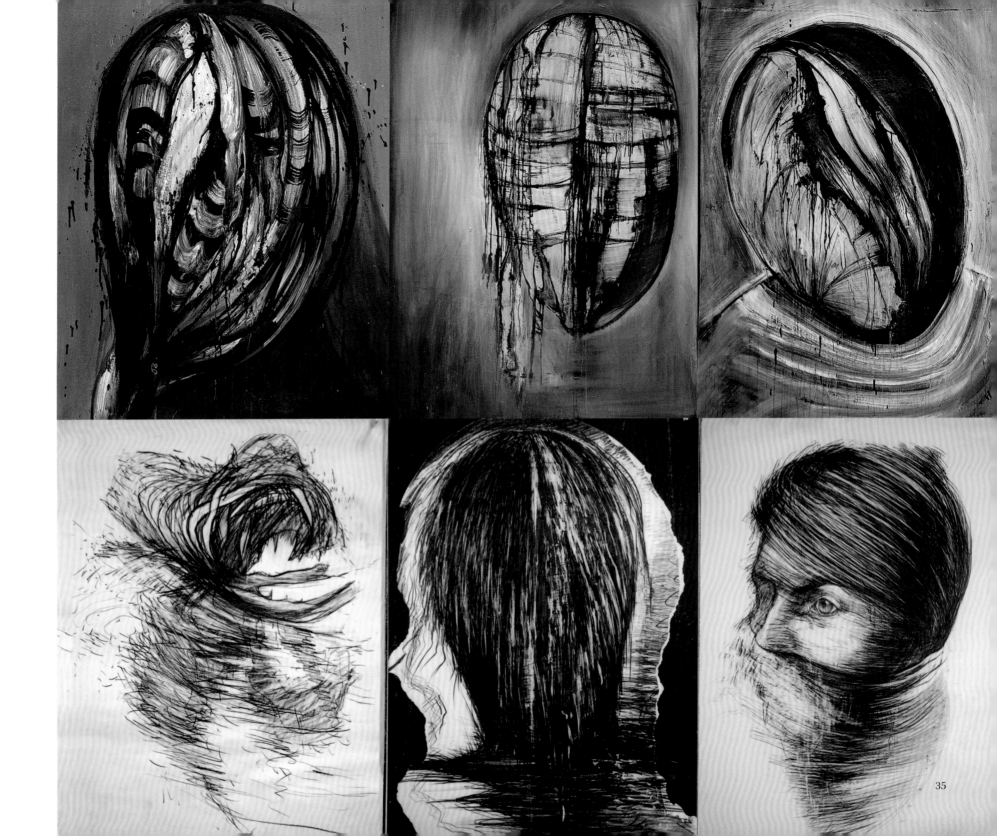

WITHDRAWN
BIOGRAPHY

1956 Graduates from Cooper Union, New York. Receives scholarship to Skowhegan School of Art, Maine

1957 Completes post graduate study in painting Cranbrook Academy, Michigan

1958 Exhibits at Camino Gallery, New York City

1959 Exhibits at Allan Stone Gallery, New York City

1961 Receives B.A. in Art Education from City College of New York

1965 Consults with Louis Kahn on Battery Park Holocaust Memorial

1967-71 Becomes resident teacher in Florence, Italy, in the California State University art program (1967-70) and in New York University's Continuing Education Department (1971)

1973 Design consultant to the President's Commission for a Holocaust Museum

1979 Exhibits at the Florence Biennale, Palazzo Strozzi

1980 Exhibits at Camden Arts Centre, London

1987-88 Consults with Jewish Museum on its exhibition "Gardens and Ghettos"

1988 Receives commission for the lobby of Hadassah House, New York City

1994 Exhibits at Pleiades Gallery, New York

1995-2000 Works with Italian craftsmen in Venice and Florence, returning to Italy periodically

1998 Opens Port Washington studio and begins working on large scale whale and tree series.

2002 Exhibits at Yeshiva University Museum, New York.

Additional information **www.lmeiselman.com**

36

Icon, 1999.
Pencil, 38x50 in.

X-Wife, III, 1997.
Pencil, 38x50 in.

PHOTO IMAGING
Karen Luckey

BOOK DESIGN
Francesca Richer

PRINTED BY
Meridian Printing

PUBLISHED BY
Violen, Inc., NY

© Leonard Meiselman 2002
All rights reserved.

ISBN # 0 - 945447 - 13 - 2

ACKNOWLEDGMENTS

I would like to thank the following for their encouragement and support: Violet Brandwein, Allan Chasanoff, Ken Eason, Ellen Fecteau, Alan Goerlick, Marilyn Goldstein, Carole Kismaric, Donald Kuspit, Dr. Max Meiselman, Jeff Schlanger, Larry Snow, Roslyn Snow